The Ultimate Sandwich Recipe Book

50 Unique Sandwich Recipes That Will
Amaze Everyone

BY: Valeria Ray

DELICIOUS
HOMEMADE
FOOD

Recipes

License Notes

A Special Reward for Purchasing My Book!

Thank you, cherished reader, for purchasing my book and taking the time to read it. As a special reward for your decision, I would like to offer a gift of free and discounted books directly to your inbox. All you need to do is fill in the box below with your email address and name to start getting amazing offers in the comfort of your own home. You will never miss an offer because a reminder will be sent to you. Never miss a deal and get great deals without having to leave the house! Subscribe now and start saving!

https://valeria-ray.gr8.com

Contents

Unique Sandwich Recipes

MMMMMMMMMMMMMMMMMMMMMMMMMMMMMMMM

(1) Spinach Sandwich with Caramelized Onions

Any recipe with caramelized onions is usually lovely. This recipe is quite tasking to make, but very rewarding at the end. Really blends well with the manouri and pepper spicing.

Serving Size: Makes 2-4 servings.

List of Ingredients:

- 2 large Caramelized Sweet Onions
- 1 giant bunch of spinach, weight is a pound or more, cut stem with very clean leaves
- Freshly ground pepper and natural salt
- 2 red peppers (meaty roasted)
- 1 slice of bread for each person, ciabatta, rye or whole grain bread
- 1 halved garlic clove
- Manouri or ricotta salata, diced thinly
- Olive oil, to complete

MMMMMMMMMMMMMMMMMMMMMMMMMMMMMMMMMM

Instructions:

1. Heat the caramelized onions in a pot at low heat.

2. Wilt the spinach in the water around the leaves in another pot and season with salt and pepper.

3. Cut the peppers into wide pieces.

4. Toast the bread, then paste one side with the garlic. Put the onions on top, then spinach, followed by the cheese and then the roasted pepper; let it be diagonally across the top.

5. Season with salt and pepper, and slightly sprinkle with olive oil

(2) Steak Sandwich Italian Style

For a fast and tasty lunch, combine this sandwich with some carrot sticks and a salad.

Serving Size: Makes 4 servings

List of Ingredients:

- 2 tablespoons olive oil
- 2 tablespoons minced garlic
- 1/8 teaspoons crushed red pepper flakes
- ½ pound of deli sliced roast beef
- ½ cup + 2 tablespoons beef broth
- 2 teaspoons dried parsley
- 2 teaspoons dried basil
- ¼ teaspoons salt (optional)
- ¼ teaspoons dried oregano
- 1/8 teaspoons ground black pepper
- 4 sandwich rolls, split
- 4 slices of provolone cheese

MMMMMMMMMMMMMMMMMMMMMMMMMMMMMMMM

Instructions:

1. In large skillet, heat oil over medium high heat.

2. Add garlic and pepper flakes; cook and stir for 1 minute.

3. Add roast beef, broth and remainder of seasonings; heat through.

4. Place beef slices on rolls.

5. Drizzle with broth mixture and top with cheese.

6. Top with roll.

7. Serve as desired.

(3) Special Egg Sandwiches Recipe

Tartar sauce gives these little egg salad sandwiches a slightly sweet flavor. Cut into bell shapes with olive "clappers," they look festive for Christmas.

Serving Size: Makes 8 servings.

List of Ingredients:

- 5 cooked and crumbled bacon strips
- 4 chopped well cooked eggs
- 2 tablespoons softened butter
- 16 slices pimiento-stuffed olives
- ¼ cup tartar sauce
- 16 slices of bread

MMMMMMMMMMMMMMMMMMMMMMMMMMMMMMMMMMMM

Instructions:

1. Mix the eggs, bacon and tartar sauce together in a bowl.

2. Cover well and refrigerate for 30 minutes.

3. Cut out two bells from each slice of bread using a cutter.

4. Spread one side of each bell with butter slightly.

5. Spread egg mixture over half of buttered bells and top with the remaining bells, buttered side down.

6. Garnish each sandwich with olive slice covering with a small amount of egg mixture.

7. Cover and refrigerate till ready for serving.

(4) Chicken Pesto Sandwiches

These are such easy sandwiches that you can serve them for parties or even a game day! They are tasty as well as simple. Chicken Pesto Sandwiches are a great make-ahead food.

Serving Size: Makes 6 servings

List of Ingredients:

- 6 boneless, skinless chicken breast halves (about 4 oz each)
- ¾ cup of prepared pesto
- ½ teaspoons salt
- ¼ teaspoons pepper
- 12 slices of Italian bread, toasted
- 1 (12oz) jar of roasted sweet red peppers, drained
- ¼ pound of sliced mozzarella cheese

MMMMMMMMMMMMMMMMMMMMMMMMMMMMMMMMMMM

Instructions:

1. Flatten the chicken to ¼" thickness.

2. Spread 1 tablespoon of pesto over each chicken breast.

3. Sprinkle with salt and pepper.

4. Grill chicken and cover with the lid, over medium heat for about 3-5 mins on both sides.

5. Spread 3 tablespoons pesto over six slices of toasted bread.

6. Layer each slice of toasted bread with red peppers, chicken and cheese.

7. Spread the remaining pesto over the remaining toasted bread; place over the top of the chicken.

(5) Quickie Gruyere Sandwich

Bacon naturally helps enhance moods and positive mental state. This sandwich is designed to help strengthen the heart. If nicely prepared using the gruyere cheese, the sandwich looks very appealing.

Serving Size: Makes 1 serving.

List of Ingredients:

- 3 toasted slices of white bread
- Cooked beef or cooked bacon
- Sliced gruyere cheese
- Lettuce, as preferred
- Toasted turkey ham, as preferred
- Vine tomato
- Mayonnaise, as required
- Salt to taste

MMMMMMMMMMMMMMMMMMMMMMMMMMMMMMM

Instructions:

1. Use a toaster to slightly toast the bread slices.

2. On one slice of the toast, spread mayonnaise.

3. Top with dices of turkey ham or bacon, vine tomatoes, cheese and lettuce.

4. Season with salt.

5. Cut into nice triangles.

6. Repeat also for the other slices.

7. Serve with French fries (potato chips) and a cup of any juice.

(6) Open-faced Tomato Sandwich

There is nothing better than a sandwich made with fresh vegetables. And it's good for you too.

Serving Size: 1-2 servings

List of Ingredients:

- 1 English Muffin, sliced in half and toasted
- 2 tablespoons of pesto of choice
- 4 slices of red onion
- 4 tomato slices, sliced about ¼" thick
- Olive oil
- Salt and pepper to taste

MMMMMMMMMMMMMMMMMMMMMMMMMMMMMMMMMM

Instructions:

1. Spread about 1 tablespoon pesto on each half of the toasted English muffin.

2. Layer 2 slices of red onion and 2 slices of tomato on top of the pesto on each muffin half.

3. Drizzle the top with a bit of olive oil; sprinkle salt and pepper to taste.

4. Serve as desired.

(7) Big Pan Bagnat

Attractive and easy to prepare. With the eggs cooked hard enough and the fresh spinach laid properly beneath the tuna mixture spread, a sweet sandwich is always the result. A very excellent recipe of all times.

Serving Size: Makes 4 servings.

List of Ingredients:

- ¼ thinly sliced sweet onion
- ¼ cup extra virgin olive oil
- 2 tablespoons red wine vinegar
- Canned Tuna (7 oz)
- ¼ cup chopped black olives
- 1 round bread (about 7 inches)
- 1 plum tomato, thinly sliced
- 1 cup packed fresh spinach
- 2 sliced hard cooked eggs
- 2 tablespoons Dijon mustard
- 1 teaspoon dried thyme
- ¼ teaspoons salt to taste
- ¼ teaspoons pepper
- 2 jarred- drained, rinsed and patted dry roasted red peppers,

MMMMMMMMMMMMMMMMMMMMMMMMMMMMMMMMMM

Instructions:

1. Put onion in cold water and cover for 15 minutes. Drain and pat dry.

2. In another bowl, mix together oil, vinegar, mustard, thyme, salt and pepper.

3. Transfer all minus 2 tablespoons to separate bowl, add tuna and olives and toss to mix.

4. Horizontally cut bread in half, hollow out loaf, leaving 1 inch border out then brush cut side with remaining oil mixture.

5. Spread tuna mixture over the bottom half of loaf, add tomato, spinach, eggs, onion and red peppers. Top with remaining bread then cut into wedges.

(8) Sloppy Buffalo Chicken Sandwiches

If the title includes the word 'sloppy,' you are sure to like it.

Serving Size: Makes 6 servings

List of Ingredients:

- 1 (8 oz) can of tomato sauce
- ¼-½ cup hot sauce
- 1 ¼-1 ½ pounds cooked chicken (leftover chick or prepackaged), chopped
- 1 loaf (16 oz) loaf of Italian bread
- 1 ½ cup Monterey Jack cheese, shredded
- ½ cup blue cheese crumbles
- Optional
- Blue Cheese Dressing, for dipping

MMMMMMMMMMMMMMMMMMMMMMMMMMMMMMMMMM

Instructions:

1. Preheat oven to 350 degrees.

2. In a large bowl, mix the tomato sauce, hot sauce and chicken.

3. Stir in the cheese until it is mixed well.

4. Slice open the loaf of bread lengthwise and fill with the chicken mixture.

5. Wrap the entire loaf sandwich tightly in foil.

6. Bake wrapped loaf on a cookie sheet in the oven for 30-45 minutes or until hot and gooey in the center.

7. Slice and serve with Blue Cheese dressing if desired.

(9) Caper Mayo and Chicken Sandwich

This chewy and nutritious easy to make sandwich is complemented with some juicy lemon drink. It's a good match for any kind of appetite in the afternoon. 'Yummy' is the best description.

Serving Size: Makes 4 servings.

List of Ingredients:

- ¼ cup extra-virgin olive oil
- 1 tablespoon grated lemon rind
- 4 boneless, skinless chicken breasts
- 1 baguette
- 3 tablespoons lemon juice
- 1 minced garlic clove
- Caper Mayonnaise
- ¼ cup light mayonnaise
- 2 tablespoons chopped fresh parsley
- 2 tablespoons drained, rinsed and chopped capers
- 1 teaspoon dried dillweed
- ¼ teaspoons salt
- ¼ teaspoons pepper
- 8 leaves lettuce
- 2 tomatoes, sliced
- 2 teaspoons lemon juice

MMMMMMMMMMMMMMMMMMMMMMMMMMMMMMMMMM

Instructions:

1. Whisk oil, lemon rind and juice, garlic, dillweed, salt and pepper together in a bowl.

2. Add chicken and turn leaving to stand for 10 minutes then refrigerate for up to 4 hours.

3. In a bowl, mix mayonnaise, capers, parsley and lemon juice.

4. At about medium-high heat, place chicken on grill turning once for about 12 minutes, until it's not pink inside anymore.

5. Dice the baguette in half lengthwise and cut crosswise into quarters. Put lettuce on bottom halves and also add tomatoes, chicken and caper mayonnaise. Cover with tops of baguette.

(10) Chicken and Pepper Sandwich

Super simple recipe for an awesome sandwich. A great way to use up leftover chicken.

Serving Size: Makes 6-8 servings

List of Ingredients:

- 1 ½ pounds of cooked chicken, shredded (can be leftovers or precooked)
- 1 of each bell pepper (red, yellow and green) cut into strips
- 1 small onion, chopped
- ¾ cup of balsamic vinaigrette dressing
- 8 whole wheat hamburger buns

MMMMMMMMMMMMMMMMMMMMMMMMMMMMMMMMMM

Instructions:

1. In a large skillet over medium heat, sauté the onions and peppers until tender.

2. Add the chicken and ½ cup of dressing to the skillet; toss well.

3. Continue cooking, stirring often, until chicken is heated through.

4. Toast the buns if desired

5. Spoon chicken mixture onto bottom bun; add more dressing if desired.

(11) Tenderloin with Lettuce Leaf Sandwiches

A lovely and healthy sandwich recipe any day any time. The tenderloins give high quality proteins and several different minerals. It surely brings nice Referrals! But ensure you mix Ingredients well.

Serving Size: Makes 6 servings.

List of Ingredients:

- ½ teaspoon ground mustard
- 2 tablespoons of sodium soy sauce
- 2 tablespoons steak sauce
- ½ teaspoon diced fresh ginger root
- 2 tablespoons, canola oil
- 2 minced garlic cloves
- 1-½ teaspoons brown sugar
- 6 lettuce leaves
- ½ teaspoon Dijon mustard
- ½ teaspoon prepared horseradish
- 2 pork tenderloins
- ¼ cup fat-free mayonnaise
- ¼ cup reduced-fat sour cream
- 1-½ teaspoons lemon juice
- 1 teaspoon sugar
- ½ teaspoon ground mustard
- 6 split kaiser rolls

MMMMMMMMMMMMMMMMMMMMMMMMMMMMMMMM

Instructions:

1. Mix the canola oil, sodium soy sauce, garlic cloves, steak sauce, brown sugar, ground mustard and gingerroot together in a medium size bowl.

2. Put into the mixture, the pork, seal bag and turn for coating leaving in the refrigerator for 8 hours.

3. Remove the marinade as you drain pork. Spread oil on grill rack to lightly coat and grill pork for 25-40 minutes at medium heat then slice after 5 minutes.

4. Gently mix the mayonnaise, sour cream, sugar, lemon juice, ground mustard, horseradish and Dijon mustard then serve pork with lettuce and mustard horseradish sauce.

(12) Thanksgiving in a Sandwich

This is a flavorful way to use up Thanksgiving leftovers. This sandwich has all the flavor of the meal in one sandwich.

Serving Size: Makes 1 servings

List of Ingredients:

- 1 ½ oz goat cheese
- 2 tablespoons of prepared pesto
- 1 ½ oz of turkey
- 1-2 tablespoons of jellied cranberry sauce
- 2 slices of thin bread
- 1-2 tablespoons butter, softened

MMMMMMMMMMMMMMMMMMMMMMMMMMMMMMMMMM

Instructions:

1. Spread the butter on the outside of both bread slices.

2. One the other side of one slice of bread, spread 1 tablespoon pesto.

3. On the other side of the other slice of bread, spread cranberry sauce.

4. Layer goat cheese and turkey; top with bread slice.

5. Cook on a hot griddle over medium heat for 3-4 minutes on each side until golden brown.

6. Serve as desired.

(13) Cilantro and Slaw Chicken Sandwich

This beauty and colorfully sauced crunchy slaw makes turns this sandwich into a regular in parties and a high demand by party-goers. A commendable blend of bright colors. Don't miss it out in your next party's menu!

Serving Size: Makes 8 servings.

List of Ingredients:

- ¼ teaspoon lime juice
- ¼ cup reduced-fat sour cream
- ½ teaspoon grated lime peel
- 1 cup broccoli coleslaw mix
- 2 tablespoons chopped finely sweet onion
- 2 tablespoons chopped finely sweet red pepper
- ¼ teaspoon salt to taste
- ½ teaspoon chili powder
- 2 tablespoons minced fresh cilantro
- ¼ teaspoon coarsely ground pepper
- 2 teaspoons lime juice
- 2 teaspoons chopped finely seeded jalapeno pepper
- 4 boneless skinless chicken breast halves (4 ounces each)
- 1 teaspoon sugar
- 8 Hawaiian sweet split rolls
- ½ teaspoon ground cumin
- 8 dices of tomato
- 8 lettuce leaves

MMMMMMMMMMMMMMMMMMMMMMMMMMMMMMMMMM

Instructions:

1. In a medium size bowl, mix the sour cream, lime juice and lime peel. In another medium bowl, mix slaw ingredients. Chill sauce and slaw until you serve.

2. Dice each chicken breast into half widthwise, make it flat to ½-in. thickness and add seasonings.

3. Rub oil on grill rack using long-handled tongs to coat lightly. Grill chicken at over medium heat for 4-7 minutes keeping it covered on each side.

4. Grill rolls for 30-60 seconds and cut sides or until toasted. Serve the chicken on rolls with tomato, lettuce, slaw and sauce.

(14) Pizza in a Sandwich

Pizza is everyone's favorite food so why not incorporate a favorite dish into a sandwich? This is a real tummy-pleaser.

Serving Size: Makes 4 servings

List of Ingredients:

- 8 slices of Italian bread, ¾" thick
- 8 slices of mozzarella cheese
- 8 slices of tomato
- 4 teaspoons parmesan cheese, grated
- ¼ teaspoons garlic salt
- 24 slices of pepperoni
- ¼ cup butter, softened
- 1 (16 oz) jar pizza sauce, warmed

MMMMMMMMMMMMMMMMMMMMMMMMMMMMMMM

Instructions:

1. On 4 slices of bread layer 1 slice mozzarella, 2 slices tomato, 1 teaspoon parmesan, dash of garlic salt and 6 slices of pepperoni.

2. Top with 1 slice of mozzarella and bread.

3. Butter the outside top and bottom of sandwich.

4. Toast sandwich on hot griddle for about 3-4 minutes on each side or until bread is brown and crispy, and the cheese is gooey.

5. Serve with warmed pizza sauce.

(15) Barbecued Turkey with Wheat Buns

Creative way of making barbecued turkey blending extra ordinarily well in sandwiches with unsweetened pineapple juice. What a dinner! They have an amazing great flavor and you'd almost never believe they were made with ground turkey.

Serving Size: Makes 6 servings.

List of Ingredients:

- 1 pound lean ground turkey
- 1 can (6 ounces) tomato paste
- ½ cup chopped onion
- ½ cup chopped green pepper
- 1 can (6 ounces) unsweetened pineapple juice
- ½ teaspoon fine garlic powder
- ½ teaspoon salt
- 1/8 teaspoon pepper
- 6 split and toasted whole wheat buns
- ¼ cup of fresh water
- 2 teaspoons Dijon mustard

MMMMMMMMMMMMMMMMMMMMMMMMMMMMMMMMMMMM

Instructions:

1. Combine the turkey, onion and green pepper and cook over medium heat in a saucepan coated with cooking spray until the meat changes from pink and drain.

2. Stir in the tomato paste, pineapple juice, salt, mustard, garlic powder, water and pepper. Then boil under reduced heat uncovered for 20-30 minutes to make sauce thickened.

3. Put 1/3 cup onto each bun.

(16) English Muffin Breakfast

Breakfast is the most important meal of the day and is often skipped because of a time or schedule crunch. These are perfect for that make-ahead, grab-and-go breakfast sandwich so that you won't have to skip the meal.

Serving Size: Makes 1 servings

List of Ingredients:

- 1 egg, fried hard with yolk broken
- 1 sausage patty or 3 strips bacon or 1 slice of ham, cooked
- 1 slice of cheese of American cheese
- 1 English muffin, toasted

MMMMMMMMMMMMMMMMMMMMMMMMMMMMMMMMMM

Instructions:

1. On bottom half of English Muffin, layer fried egg, cooked breakfast meat and top with slice of cheese.

2. Replace top.

3. Serve as desired.

(17) Strawberry and Turkey Sandwich

A very tasty sandwich even a 6th grade can put together. Fresh strawberries really make this a unique tasting sandwich.

Serving Size: Makes 2 servings.

List of Ingredients:

- 2 fresh lettuce leaves
- 4 slices whole wheat bread
- 2 slices reduced-fat cheese
- 2 tablespoons reduced-fat soft cream cheese
- 2 teaspoons finely chopped pecans
- ¼ pound thinly sliced turkey breast
- 4 sliced fresh strawberries

MMMMMMMMMMMMMMMMMMMMMMMMMMMMMMMMMM

Instructions:

1. Layer the lettuce, cheese, turkey and strawberries on the slices of bread.

2. Mix cream cheese and pecans and spread over the remaining bread.

3. Place over strawberries

(18) Po'Boy

Louisiana-style cooking in a sandwich. A traditional Po'Boy contains the previous day's meat and cheese from the butcher.

Serving Size: Makes 4 servings

List of Ingredients:

- 1 pound of packaged spicy popcorn chicken
- 2 cups prepared coleslaw
- Dash of crushed red pepper
- 4 sesame seed hoagie buns, toasted

MMMMMMMMMMMMMMMMMMMMMMMMMMMMMMMMMMMM

Instructions:

1. Prepare popcorn chicken as per package instructions.

2. Spread ½ cup of prepared coleslaw on each bottom half of the toasted hoagie rolls.

3. Sprinkle with crushed red pepper as desired.

4. Arrange popcorn chicken over each bottom roll on top of coleslaw.

5. Place top bun on chicken.

6. Serve as desired.

(19) Spicy Lamb Sandwich

These fine sandwiches will definitely become the talk of any get-together. Sourdough baguettes with cucumber, cheese, marinated lamb and artichokes all in a sandwich is just and mouthwatering and CLASSY!

Serving Size: Makes 24 servings.

List of Ingredients:

- Lemon juice
- 6 minced garlic cloves
- Olive oil (2 spoons)
- 1 boneless leg of lamb
- Artichoke hearts
- 2 tablespoons minced fresh rosemary
- 1 teaspoon salt
- ¼ teaspoon cayenne pepper
- Tomatoes (2)
- 6 tablespoonss. of vinaigrette
- 2 sourdough baguettes
- 1 thinly sliced cucumber
- 1 pack, sliced goat cheese

MMMMMMMMMMMMMMMMMMMMMMMMMMMMMMMMMM

Instructions:

1. Combine the lemon juice, cup olive oil, garlic cloves, rosemary, salt and cayenne pepper in a plastic bag.

2. Add the lamb, seal bag and turn to coat. Then put in the fridge for 8 hours.

3. Drain the marinade, roast lamb in a pan and bake openly for 80-90 minutes at 325°. Leave to cool over and refrigerate for at least 2 hours.

4. Place artichokes in a plastic bag and add 2/3 cup of vinaigrette.

5. Tightly seal the bag and turn to coat. Leave it for 10 minutes. Then drain and discard marinade.

6. Thinly slice the lamb, cutting each baguette in half horizontally. Gently hollow out the top and bottom, leaving a about ¾-in shell.

7. Rub the bottom half of each loaf with 2 tablespoons vinaigrette, put cucumber, lamb, tomatoes and artichokes, then gently drizzle with the left vinaigrette. Add the goat cheese.

8. Replace the bread tops and firmly press down. Now wrap tightly in plastic bags before refrigerating for at least 2 hours. Cut them as needed

(20) The Dagwood

We all remember Dagwood Bumstead, right? He was the guy who came home to fix a snack and ended up emptying the whole fridge onto his bread. And how he got that sandwich in his mouth is a miracle. This sandwich will remind you of those days of the cartoon.

Serving Size: 5 servings

List of Ingredients:

- 10 slices of a crusty white bread, sliced
- Assorted fresh greens (leaf, Romaine, Red Leaf, etc.)
- ¼ pound each of thinly sliced pepper jack cheese, white American cheese, provolone cheese and cheddar cheese
- ¼ pound each of thinly sliced deli meats: turkey, pastrami, salami, ham, pepperoni and roast beef
- 1 large beefsteak tomato, sliced
- ½ large yellow pepper, thinly sliced
- 4 slices of bacon, crisply cooked

MMMMMMMMMMMMMMMMMMMMMMMMMMMMMMMM

Instructions:

1. Lay out 5 slices of bread.

2. Layer 2 with green leaf lettuce.

3. Layer each of the remaining 3 slices with other greens.

4. Layer the first green leaf sandwich with 3 slices of pepper jack cheese, turkey and 4 slices of tomato.

5. Cover with another slice of bread.

6. Place on a spindle.

7. Layer 2nd green leaf sandwich half with 3 white American cheese slices; add pastrami and top with slice of bread.

8. Place on spindle on top of other sandwich.

9. Take another lettuce half and place 3 slices of provolone; add 2 slices of salami and 1 slice of ham folded in half, 2 slices of pepperoni, another slice of ham, folded and top with yellow peppers and bread slice.

10. Place sandwich on spindle with other sandwiches.

11. Next lettuce half, place 3 slices cheddar, 2 slices of tomato, fold entire ¼ pound of roast beef and add to sandwich.

12. Top with bread slice and add to other sandwiches on spindle.

13. Take last lettuce half and add 3 slices tomato and 4 slices of bacon; top with bread.

14. Place last sandwich on spindle with other sandwiches.

15. Serve as desired.

(21) Visible Roast Beef Sandwich

Fresh arugula and romaine mixed in between ciabatta bread slices is simply mouth-watering. Nice arrangement and superb selection of compatible ingredients.

Serving Size: Makes 8 servings.

List of Ingredients:

- 1 pound sliced deli roast beef
- 2 cups fresh arugula
- 8 slices ciabatta bread
- 1 tablespoon white wine vinegar
- 1-½ tablespoons prepared horseradish
- 2 cups torn romaine
- 4 teaspoons olive oil
- 1 tablespoon lemon juice

MMMMMMMMMMMMMMMMMMMMMMMMMMMMMMMMMMM

Instructions:

1. Nicely arrange the roast beef on ciabatta slices as you will.

2. Combine all the arugula and romaine in a bowl.

3. Whisk the remaining ingredientsin another bowl until it's blended.

4. Sprinkle over the greens and toss to coat. Nicely arrange over beef and serve immediately.

(22) Monte Cristo with Bacon

The perfect deep fried sandwich and bacon too? Sounds delicious right? This sandwich can be cut in half for a regular meal serving, or you can make it in batches to cut into quarters for finger sandwiches for parties and get-togethers.

Serving Size: 4 servings

List of Ingredients:

- 8 slices thick cut bacon, cooked
- 8 slices of whole wheat bread
- 8 slices of deli ham
- 8 slices of cheese of choice
- 2-4 tablespoons butter, softened
- 3 eggs
- ¼ cup milk
- Salt, to taste

MMMMMMMMMMMMMMMMMMMMMMMMMMMMMMMMM

Instructions:

1. Lay out the 8 slices of bread.

2. Lightly spread butter on all 8 slices of bread.

3. Lay 1 slice of cheese on each bread slice.

4. Place 1 slice of ham onto each cheese slice.

5. Cut the cooked bacon in half and place 4 halves of bacon on 4 stacks.

6. Put bottom sandwich onto stacks.

7. Cut crust off of each of the 4 sandwiches.

8. Wrap sandwich in plastic wrap and refrigerate for 30 minutes.

9. In a mixing bowl, combine milk and eggs.

10. Heat griddle over medium-high heat.

11. Brush griddle with softened butter.

12. Unwrap sandwich and dip into egg batter; coat evenly.

13. Gently place sandwich on griddle and fry.

14. Turn once and cover with a glass bowl until golden brown and hot for about 5 minutes total.

15. Remove from heat.

16. Serve as desired.

(23) Swordfish Sandwiches

I love this sandwich and I nicknamed it, the hunger-killer. Gingery swordfish steak on a sandwich.

Serving Size: Makes 4 servings.

List of Ingredients:

- 4 swordfish steaks (5 ounces each)
- 1 cup canned bean sprouts
- ¼ cup red onion, thinly sliced
- 8 teaspoons zero-free blue cheese salad dressing
- ¾ cup julienned carrots
- ½ teaspoon diced fresh ginger root
- 1 tablespoon lime juice
- 1 teaspoon sugar
- 1/8 teaspoon cayenne pepper
- 4 slices toasted bread
- 1 tablespoon olive oil
- ½ teaspoon salt

MMMMMMMMMMMMMMMMMMMMMMMMMMMMMMMMM

Instructions:

1. Put the bean sprouts, carrots and onion in a bowl and mix well.

2. Add the lime juice, sugar and ginger, stirring into vegetable mixture. Then cover and refrigerate for 30 minutes.

3. Sprinkle both sides of swordfish steaks with oil, then with salt and cayenne.

4. Lightly coat the grill rack with cooking oil.

5. Uncover and grill fish at medium-hot heat for 4-6 minutes on each side.

6. Nicely lay a swordfish steak on each piece of toast; top with 2 teaspoons blue cheese dressing and about ½ cup bean sprout mixture.

(24) Turkey Salad with a Kick

This turkey salad gives a bit of a different taste using chipotle (smoked, dried jalapenos) powder for a new flavor. This turkey salad can be used for sandwiches, as a dip with crackers or on a bed of lettuce.

Serving Size: Makes enough for 2 sandwiches

List of Ingredients:

- 1 cup of cooked turkey, chopped
- ¼ cup onion, chopped
- ¼ cup celery, chopped
- 1 tablespoon jalapeno pepper, chopped
- 1 tablespoon cilantro leaves
- ¼ cup of mayonnaise
- ¼ teaspoons chipotle powder
- Salt and pepper to taste
- 4 slices whole wheat bread

Optional toppings

- Sliced avocado
- Sliced tomatoes

MMMMMMMMMMMMMMMMMMMMMMMMMMMMMMMMMMMM

Instructions:

1. In a small bowl, mix chipotle powder into the mayonnaise; set aside.

2. In a large mixing bowl, put turkey, onion, celery, jalapenos and cilantro together.

3. Fold in lightly the mayonnaise seasoned with chipotle into the turkey mixture.

4. Add salt and pepper to taste.

5. Spoon mixture onto bread slices

6. Top with tomato and avocado slices, if desired.

7. Cut sandwich in half.

8. Serve.

(25) Portabella Bacon Sandwich

With the world becoming a bit more health-conscious, people are trying to cut back on their carb intake. Here is a new take on the sandwich minus the bread.

Serving Size: 2 servings

List of Ingredients:

- 4 Portabella Mushroom caps
- 2 tablespoons canola oil
- 1 boneless and skinless chicken cutlet, cooked and cut into 2 pieces
- 2 slices of tomato
- ½ cup of fresh spinach leaves
- 2 slices of cooked bacon of choice
- 3 tablespoons guacamole

MMMMMMMMMMMMMMMMMMMMMMMMMMMMMMM

Instructions:

1. Scoop or cut out the gills and stem from the mushroom.

2. Heat oil in a pan and cook mushrooms for 3-5 mins on both sides or until they turn tender and golden brown on top.

3. Remove the mushrooms from the pan.

4. On one mushroom, layer on the cooked chicken, bacon, tomato, spinach and 1 ½ tablespoons guacamole.

5. Top with another mushroom cap.

6. Repeat with other 2 mushroom caps.

7. Serve as desired.

(26) Peanut Butter Apple Sandwich

As children, we adored peanut butter sandwiches. For some, a large part of our childhood was spent eating peanut butter because we just simply did not want to eat anything else. Peanut butter is good and good for you. This sandwich gives a new twist to a childhood favorite.

Serving Size: Makes 4 sandwiches

List of Ingredients:

- 1 large apple of choice
- Peanut butter of choice
- 8 slices of whole wheat bread

MMMMMMMMMMMMMMMMMMMMMMMMMMMMMMMMMMMM

Instructions:

1. Core the apple.

2. Cut the apple into quarters and slice.

3. Spread peanut butter on bread slices. Make sure you spread the peanut butter all the way to the sides of the bread. Use a generous amount so that the apple slices stick.

4. Put slices of apple over the peanut butter in a single layer.

5. Top with another slice of bread that has had peanut butter spread onto it.

6. Cut sandwich in half.

7. Serve.

(27) Italian Turkey Sandwich

The tasty and crunchiness sends one's imagination to fantasy land. Turkey breast combines very well with onions and pepper giving it a perfect finishing

Serving Size: Makes 12 servings.

List of Ingredients:

- 1 chopped medium onion
- 1 bone-in turkey breast (6 pounds) without skin
- 2 tablespoons dried Italian seasoning
- 4 teaspoons beef bouillon granules
- 12 split kaiser
- 1 chopped small green pepper
- ¼ cup chili sauce
- 3 tablespoons white vinegar

MMMMMMMMMMMMMMMMMMMMMMMMMMMMMMMMMM

Instructions:

1. In a greased low heat cooker, place turkey breast. Add onion and green pepper in a pan.

2. Add the chili sauce, Italian seasoning, vinegar and bouillon.

3. Put it over turkey and vegetables, cover and cook on low heat until turkey is tender.

4. Nicely shred the turkey with two forks and return to the low heat cooker. Spoon ½ cup on each bread.

(28) Outside in Sandwiches

Looking for something quick and tasty for lunch? Something you could just grab and go with? Well, look no further. This is a neat twist on the old sandwich. This sandwich makes for a quick snack or a fast lunch while on-the-go.

Serving Size: 8 servings

List of Ingredients:

- 6oz deli ham, thinly sliced
- 8 slices of American cheese
- 8 slices of whole wheat sandwich bread, crusts removed
- ½ cup of mayonnaise
- 8 dill pickle spears

MMMMMMMMMMMMMMMMMMMMMMMMMMMMMMMMMM

Instructions:

1. Divide ham into 8 portions.

2. Top each stack with one slice of American cheese.

3. Spread mayonnaise on both sides of each slice of bread.

4. Place one slice of bread on each ham and cheese stack.

5. Trim ham to fit sides of bread.

6. Place a dill pickle spear in the center of each stack.

7. Roll stacks tightly.

8. Wrap in plastic wrap.

9. Refrigerate overnight.

(29) Cucumber Deli Subs

These subs are filled with crunchy goodness. They are also suited for those who are more health conscious.

Serving Size: 4 servings

List of Ingredients:

- 2 large cucumbers
- ¼ pound deli meat of choice (turkey, chicken, roast beef, etc.)
- ¼ pound deli cheese of choice (Swiss, Cheddar, Provolone, etc.)
- 2-4 tablespoons low fat ranch dressing
- Optional toppings
- Tomatoes
- Lettuce
- Pepper slices

MMMMMMMMMMMMMMMMMMMMMMMMMMMMMMMMMMM

Instructions:

1. Peel cucumbers

2. Remove a thin slice lengthwise from the side of the cucumber to prevent it from rolling.

3. Scoop out the seeds and discard.

4. Separate each cucumber into half.

5. Fill 2 cucumber halves with half of the deli meat and half of the cheese.

6. Add optional toppings if desired.

7. Drizzle low fat ranch dressing over the meat, cheese and toppings.

8. Place remain 2 cucumber halves onto of the meat, cheese and topping filled cucumbers.

9. Cut in half and serve as desired.

(30) Supper Sloppy Joes

Everyone loves a good Sloppy Joe; adults and kids alike. It makes for quick and easy dinner for busy moms and it's something that the kids will eat with no arguments. This recipe is also good to make ahead and freeze for those future busy evenings.

Serving Size: 14 servings

List of Ingredients:

- 3 pounds ground beef
- 3 cups ketchup
- 2/3 cup sweet pickle relish
- 1 envelope of onion soup mix
- 14 whole wheat hamburger buns

MMMMMMMMMMMMMMMMMMMMMMMMMMMMMMMMMM

Instructions:

1. Cook ground beef in a Dutch oven over medium heat until it is no longer pink. Drain the meat.

2. Stir in the ketchup, relish and onion soup mix; heat through.

3. Spoon about ½ cup onto each bun.

4. Serve.

5. If desired, cool the mixture and freeze in freezer containers for up to 3 months.

(31) Turkey in the Garden Sandwich

A delicious sandwich with turkey breast and various garden vegetables. Nice color combination in between the bread.

Serving Size: Makes 4 servings.

List of Ingredients:

- 1-¼ cups tomatoes (chopped, seeded)
- ½ cup of fat-reduced garlic-herb spreadable cheese
- 2 bacon strips, cooked and crumbled
- 4 slices of bread
- 1-¼ cups julienned fresh spinach
- ¼ teaspoon roughly ground pepper
- ¾ cup chopped sweet red pepper
- 1 bone-in turkey breast (6 pounds) without skin

MMMMMMMMMMMMMMMMMMMMMMMMMMMMMMMMMMM

Instructions:

1. Cook turkey breast in a greased low-heat cooker.

2. Add the diced onions and green pepper.

3. Rub 2 tablespoons spreadable cheese on top of each bread.

4. Top with tomatoes, red pepper, bacon, spinach and pepper.

(32) Waffle Sandwich

A perfect sandwich for kids or even for those who are a kid at heart.

Serving Size: 1 sandwich

List of Ingredients:

- 2 Eggo Nutri-Grain Waffles
- 2 tablespoons nut butter (peanut, hazelnut, etc.)
- 1 teaspoon honey
- ½ of a banana, sliced
- 1 teaspoon butter

MMMMMMMMMMMMMMMMMMMMMMMMMMMMMMMMMM

Instructions:

1. Prepare the waffles as per the directions on package.

2. Spread 1 tablespoon of nut butter on each waffle.

3. Layer the banana slices and drizzle with honey.

4. Put the waffles together.

5. Grill on a lightly buttered hot griddle until the waffles are golden brown.

6. Serve hot.

(33) Colorful Chicken and Almond Blend Sandwich

The almonds bring a great healthy benefit to this sandwich. It helps bring relief from constipation, impotency and diabetes. Have a nice time eating this lovely meal.

Serving Size: Makes 4 servings.

List of Ingredients:

- ¼ cup diced celery
- ¼ cup sliced almonds
- ¾ cup mayonnaise
- ¼ cup golden raisins
- ¼ cup dried cranberries
- 2 cups cubed cooked chicken breast
- 4 split sweetened bread or croissants
- 2 tablespoons chopped red onion
- ¼ teaspoon pepper
- ¼ teaspoon salt, optional

MMMMMMMMMMMMMMMMMMMMMMMMMMMMMMMMMMM

Instructions:

1. Combine the diced celery, golden raisins, dried cranberries, sliced almonds, mayonnaise, red onion, pepper in a bowl and add salt if desired.

2. Stir in the chicken nicely.

3. Using a spoon, put about ½ cup into each croissant.

(34) BLT ala Chicken Salad

Chicken and bacon make for a great combination to make your mouth water. And you can't go wrong with bacon.

Serving Size: 6 servings

List of Ingredients:

- 4 pounds of cooked chicken, shredded
- 1 ½ cups mayonnaise
- 2 diced medium tomatoes
- ½ pound crumbled, cooked bacon
- 6 ciabatta buns, split
- Salt and pepper to taste
- Optional Toppings
- Lettuce
- Shredded cheese of choice

MMMMMMMMMMMMMMMMMMMMMMMMMMMMMMMMM

Instructions:

1. In a mixing bowl, combine the shredded chicken, mayonnaise, diced tomatoes and crumbled bacon.

2. Mix well.

3. Add salt and pepper to taste.

4. Toast the ciabatta buns.

5. Spoon chicken mixture onto bottom half of toasted ciabatta bun

6. Add optional toppings if desired.

7. Serve as desired.

(35) Golden Brown Baked Butternut Squash Panini

Butternut squash, also known as butternut pumpkin is a joy to behold. You'll surely love the feeling of the taste! Quite less expensive than pumpkins and easier to cook; it is a popular meal on the menu during family re-union and camp meetings.

Serving Size: Makes 4 servings.

List of Ingredients:

- 1 medium size of peeled butternut squash, diced to ¼ inch slices
- Some pepper and salt
- 1/3 c. very fresh sage, diced to flat ribbons
- 1 tablespoon olive oil and extra olive oil rub on the bread
- 1-7 oz. container fresh mozzarella medallions
- 8 large loaves of hearty whole wheat or sourdough bread (please ensure it is strong and solid)

MMMMMMMMMMMMMMMMMMMMMMMMMMMMMMMM

Instructions:

1. Raise oven temperature to 400 degrees first.

2. Rub olive oil on the sliced butternut squash and set on to a baking sheet with rim. Slightly season with pepper and salt to make it tasty.

3. Bake till it becomes golden brown or for 42-46 minutes.

4. Subject panini press to medium-high preheating.

5. Rub olive oil on a single side of each loaf of bread.

6. Equally put sage, squash and mozzarella to the part of 4 loaves of bread not oiled.

7. Top with the rest bread loaves and grill for approximately 8 minutes till it becomes golden brown

(36) Carrot and Green Bean Sandwich

Searching for a summer appetizer for lunch and evening munching? This cute piece of snack surely could be the answer. Full of color, variety of sensations on the taste bud, the carrots send the final notes: DELICIOUS!

Serving Size: Makes 4 serving.

List of Ingredients:

- 1 teaspoon yellow mustard seeds
- 3 tablespoons of water
- ¼ teaspoons salt to taste
- 2 cups trimmed green beans
- 1 cup julienned carrots
- 1/3 cup rice wine vinegar
- ¼ cup granulated sugar

MMMMMMMMMMMMMMMMMMMMMMMMMMMMMM

Instructions:

1. Toast mustard seeds in a pan over medium-high heat for 1 minute.

2. Stir in vinegar, water, sugar and salt until sugar dissolves out.

3. Boil, reducing the heat and simmer for 2 minutes.

4. Add to it, green beans and carrots.

5. Return to boil for about 2 minutes while covering until beans are soft-crispy. Allow it to cool.

6. Put in between two sliced of bread to make a sandwich

(37) Morning Toast with Pumpkin Cream Cheese

If the first meal to be served is a sandwich, then this will never disappoint. Really helps kick start the day. The vanilla extracts make it taste really cool. It's also very easy to prepare

Serving Size: Makes 1 serving.

List of Ingredients:

- 2 Medium (pumpkin flavor) Bread slices
- 1 Dash Nonstick cooking Butter
- 8 Ounce, soft Cream cheese
- ¼ Cup (Optional) Maple syrup
- ½ Teaspoon Cinnamon powder
- ½ Teaspoon Pumpkin spice blend
- ½ Cup Pumpkin puree
- ¼ Cup Brown sugar
- ½ Teaspoon Vanilla extract
- 1/3 Cup Almond coconut milk/Single cream
- 1 Large Egg
- 1/8 Teaspoon Cinnamon powder
- 1/8 Teaspoon Pumpkin spice blend
- ¼ Teaspoon Vanilla extract
- 2 Pinches Cinnamon sugar
- 1 Tablespoon Maple syrup

MMMMMMMMMMMMMMMMMMMMMMMMMMMMMMMM

Instructions:

1. Mix cream cheese, pumpkin puree, maple syrup, brown sugar, cinnamon, pumpkin spice and vanilla extract in a bowl. Stir well till combined and keep in the refrigerator first.

2. Mix milk, egg, cinnamon, pumpkin spice, vanilla extract in another bowl, stir well until the egg is mixture is fine. Set aside.

3. Spread the stuffing on 1 slice of bread leaving the edges. Place the other slice over it to make a sandwich.

4. Pour the egg wash in a large mouthed shallow plate.

5. Put the stuffed bread slices on it and roll in the egg mixture. Leave it for a few second to soak the flavors.

6. Heat a skillet and spray a non-stick spray. Set the bread slices on it and fry till browned on all sides.

7. Using two spatulas turn them over on all sides so as to cook equally.

8. Place the French toast in a serving plate, sprinkle cinnamon sugar and pour the maple syrup over it. It's set for breakfast!

(38) Refreshing and Crunchy Veggie Sandwich

With all the fresh veggies in this sandwich it will fulfill a craving for crunch. And it is certainly not lacking in taste either.

Serving Size: 1 sandwich

List of Ingredients:

- 2 slices of whole grain bread
- 2 teaspoons mayonnaise
- ½ avocado, sliced thinly
- 3-4 slices tomato
- Mixed lettuce greens of choice
- ¼ cup alfalfa sprouts
- 2-3 teaspoons salsa

MMMMMMMMMMMMMMMMMMMMMMMMMMMMMMMMMMM

Instructions:

1. Spread mayonnaise on each slice of bread.

2. Top one slice with the avocado slices, tomato, mixed greens and sprouts.

3. Top the sprouts with the salsa; then top with remaining slice of bread.

4. Cut in half and serve as desired.

(39) Sliced Onion Soup Sandwich

Fantastic meal! Difficult to resist and can be eaten severally daily. There's something magical about the combo of the onions and the broth; Takes a little more time, but worth every second!

Serving Size: Makes 4 servings.

List of Ingredients:

- 2 large onions sliced to thin sizes
- 1 c. shredded Gruyere cheese
- Pepper and salt to make tasty
- ½ teaspoons dried thyme
- 2 tablespoons olive oil
- 4 halved ciabatta rolls
- 4 c. heated broth without beef, heated (meatless beef broth)

MMMMMMMMMMMMMMMMMMMMMMMMMMMMMMMMM

Instructions:

1. In a large skillet, pour some olive and heat on low.

2. Add sliced onions and cook for approximately 1 hour 20 minutes until it is caramelized maintaining constant stirring.

3. Stop heating and mix in salt, pepper and thyme to taste.

4. Grill panini press on high or heat.

5. Separate caramelized onions to bottom of rolls and top each with ¼ cup of cheese

6. Grill for 11-16 minutes or until bread is golden-brown and the cheese is melted.

7. For each sandwich, serve with 1 cup of broth.

(40) Veggie Meatball Parm Hero

This idea of a vegetarian meatball hero is very healthy. It smoothens up the diet with meatball hero garnished with vegetable protein. The right recipe didn't take me too long to figure out. It even turned out to be a nice meal for non-vegetarians too. Yeah!

Serving Size: Makes 2 servings.

List of Ingredients:

- A pack of Gimme Lean "Ground Sausage Style"
- ½ small yellow onion, ground
- 3 tablespoons olive oil
- Cheddar cheese, about 10-12 thin slices
- ½ cup jarred marinara sauce
- 1 cup sliced crimini mushrooms
- 2 hero rolls
- Freshly chopped Parsley

MMMMMMMMMMMMMMMMMMMMMMMMMMMMMMMMMMMM

Instructions:

1. Use your hands to mix the Gimme Lean and yellow onion together till they blend.

2. Roll out into 1 ½ inch meatballs.

3. Pour the oil into a large frying pan and set over a medium-high heat. When heated, put the meatballs into the pan and cook until it one side becomes browned.

4. Use a spatula to flip over the meatballs and allow the other side brown up too. Gently toss the meatballs around in the pan till they a little color is added on all sides. Put off the burner and transfer the meatballs to a plate.

5. Put the mushrooms into the pan used to cook the meatballs and set the burner to medium-high heat. Space out the mushrooms and cook them till they become crispy outside ensuring they don't burn then transfer to a bowl.

6. To assemble the hero, cut the submarine bread into half. Line each side of the bread with 3 or 4 slices of cheddar cheese. Fill each with 5 or 6 meatballs and finely top with the marinara sauce. Add extra 2 or 3 slices of cheese to the top of the meatballs.

7. Line the baking sheet with aluminum foil and place the sandwich. Put the pan under the broiler in the oven until the cheese has melts the sandwich.

8. Withdraw the pan out of the oven and top each with mushrooms. Sprinkle chopped parsley and serve immediately.

(41) Cucumber Cream Cheese Sandwiches

This would be a perfect addition to any party or gathering. And they will give a nice little bit of class to any home party.

Serving Size: 14 servings

List of Ingredients:

- 1 thin cucumber sliced thin, each slice halved
- 1 tomato, sliced thin
- 3oz of cream cheese
- Fresh dill
- Fresh parsley
- 1 very small onion, chopped
- 1 tablespoon sugar
- ½ teaspoons salt
- Dash of pepper
- Thin sliced white bread

MMMMMMMMMMMMMMMMMMMMMMMMMMMMMMMM

Instructions:

1. Put parsley, dill and onion in a food processor and pulse until chopped fine.

2. Add the cream cheese, sugar, salt and pepper and pulse again until smooth.

3. Cut the crust off of the bread.

4. Spread the cream cheese mixture on half of the bread slices, the layer cucumber, tomato, cream cheese, and cucumber and top with another bread slice.

5. Cut sandwiches into four triangle quarters.

6. Arrange on platter and serve.

(42) Fresh Tomato and Parmesan Panini

This combination always overrates fresh tomatoes, but the final outcome can never be denied. Kudos to fresh tomatoes despite a few reservations. Then the attraction from the aroma is seals up the recipe's excellence

Serving Size: Makes 4 servings.

List of Ingredients:

To make the Roasted Tomatoes:

- 2 Roma tomatoes, diced into ¼-inch sizes
- 1 tablespoon olive oil
- 1 tablespoon balsamic vinegar
- Salt and pepper to taste
- ¼ teaspoons Italian seasoning
- To make the Tomato Pesto:
- ½ c. sun-dried tomatoes (similar to ones in a jar of oil)
- 5 basil leaves
- 1 tablespoon oil from sun-dried tomato jar
- 2 tablespoons shredded Parmesan cheese

To make the Sandwiches:

- 1 big loaf of ciabatta bread
- Tomato Pesto
- Roasted Tomatoes
- 1thinly sliced tomato
- ¼ c. basil leaves
- 4 oz. mozzarella cheese, sliced into 8 parts
- Olive oil to rub grill or panini press

MMMMMMMMMMMMMMMMMMMMMMMMMMMMMMMMMMMMM

Instructions:

Roasted Tomatoes:

1. First heat oven to about 400 degrees.

2. Line baking sheet with parchment paper and place tomato slices.

3. Sprinkle with olive oil and balsamic vinegar gently. Then with Italian seasoning, salt, and pepper.

4. Either bake for 21-26 minutes or when it softens and starts getting brown.

Tomato Pesto:

5. Add together all ingredients in food processor and start processing until it becomes smooth.

Sandwiches:

6. Grill to high heat or preheat panini press.

7. Slice ciabatta bread to 4 equal parts and then cut each part to half length. Spread tomato pesto to the bottom of each ciabatta part. Top with roasted tomatoes, fresh tomatoes, basil leaves, and mozzarella.

8. Rub grill with olive oil, place panini on the press and start heating for about 7-10 minutes to melt the cheese.

(43) Black Beans in a Bun

This is a tasty vegan sandwich that is good any time. It is simple to make yet healthy. Black Beans in a Bun can be seasoned and topped to suit your tastes. This is also a quick sandwich to make, having a total preparation and cook time of less than 30 minutes. What do you want on your black bean sandwich?

Serving Size: makes 6-8 sandwich patties, depending on size

List of Ingredients:

- ¼-½ cup onion, chopped (depending on personal taste)
- 1 tablespoon minced garlic
- 30 oz of canned black beans, rinsed and drained
- 2 tablespoons cilantro
- 2 tablespoons parsley
- 1 medium egg
- ½ teaspoons flaked red pepper
- ½ cup of bread crumbs
- 6-8 whole wheat hamburger buns

Optional Toppings

- Condiments (ketchup, mustard, mayonnaise, etc.)
- Sliced tomato
- Leaf lettuce
- Sliced onion

MMMMMMMMMMMMMMMMMMMMMMMMMMMMMMMMMMMM

Instructions:

1. Pulse onion and garlic in food processor until finely chopped.

2. Add one can of black beans to the food processor mix as well as cilantro, parsley, egg and flaked red pepper; pulse to combine ingredients.

3. Transfer mixture to a large mixing bowl.

4. Add remaining can of black beans to the mixture as well as the bread crumbs.

5. Season with pepper and mix until combined well.

6. Form mixture into patties.

7. Heat a grill pan over medium-low heat; add oil.

8. Place patties in grill pan and cook about 6 minutes on each side, or until heated through.

9. Place patty on the bottom of each bun.

10. Top with desired toppings and serve.

(44) Honey Banana Sandwich

It tastes just as the name is. Banana and honey mix flavor. Don't miss the ice cream out and ensure its vanilla. Very special meal.

Serving Size: Makes 2 serving.

List of Ingredients:

- 2 Ripe bananas
- ½ Teaspoon Cinnamon
- 1 Tablespoon Grapeseed oil or Butter
- 2 Tablespoon Honey

MMMMMMMMMMMMMMMMMMMMMMMMMMMMMMMMMMM

Instructions:

1. Peel the bananas and cut into ½ inch thick slices.

2. Subject a non-stick skillet to over medium heat and add oil or butter, honey, salt and cinnamon; then stir to dissolve.

3. Flatten the banana slices, and fry for 4-5 minutes. Be careful with the browning.

4. Serve with vanilla ice cream or layer them with peanut butter and marshmallow cream in a sandwich.

(45) Apple Nut Butter Sandwich

This sandwich is packed with protein and will help settle a grumbling tummy quickly. This is a good choice for those who are health conscious.

Serving Size: 1 serving

List of Ingredients:

- 1 large apple
- 1 ½ tablespoons nut butter (peanut, hazelnut, etc.)
- 1 teaspoon chocolate chips of choice
- 2 teaspoons raisins of choice
- 2 teaspoons peanuts (optional)

MMMMMMMMMMMMMMMMMMMMMMMMMMMMMMMMMMM

Instructions:

1. Core the apple and slice into several horizontal slices.

2. Take 2 of the slices and spread with nut butter of choice.

3. Drop the chocolate chips, raisins and peanuts on top of the nut butter.

4. Put the 2 slices together.

5. Serve as desired.

(46) Red Pepper Hummus Sandwich

A sandwich that make vegetarians smile at the first bite. The hummus and red pepper together with the spices make a super delicious sandwich.

Serving Size: Makes 2 servings.

List of Ingredients:

- 1 red bell pepper
- 1 can washed chickpeas
- 1 diced garlic clove
- ¼ teaspoon cayenne pepper
- 2 tablespoons tahini paste
- 1 tablespoon olive oil
- 2 teaspoons paprika
- 1 teaspoon fine garlic powder
- 1 teaspoon cumin powder
- Salt and pepper to make tasty
- 2 tablespoons water

MMMMMMMMMMMMMMMMMMMMMMMMMMMMMMMM

Instructions:

1. Roast at 500° F in a broiler until it is charred; keep turning for about 11 minutes.

2. Withdraw from oven to make it cool. Peel skin, remove seeds and membranes, and pat dry with any paper towel. Chop pepper roughly.

3. Add chickpeas, garlic, spices, roasted red pepper, tahini and olive oil to any food processor or fast blender to blend completely. Add 1 tablespoon of water interval if it's too thick till. Season with salt and pepper, as you will.

(47) Blueberry and Cashew Butter Sandwich

How hungry can you be after a long walk on the sand beach during a nice summer? You sure would desire the sweet taste of this blueberry jam and cashew flavor.

Serving Size: Makes 1 serving.

List of Ingredients:

- 3 pieces wheat bread
- 2 teaspoons Earth Balance Margarine
- 2 tablespoons Organic Blueberry Jam
- 1 tablespoon cashew butter

MMMMMMMMMMMMMMMMMMMMMMMMMMMMMMMMMM

Instructions:

1. Spread blueberry jam on the first piece of bread.

2. Place the second one on top of it, spread cashew butter on it and then add another spread of jam.

3. Put the third bread and spread margarine lightly on it.

4. Medium heat the frying pan and put sandwich on it with the margarine side down.

5. Now also spread the top of the bread with margarine and grill on each side until it is golden brown and serve immediately.

(48) Fruit Peanut Butter Sandwich

Fruit sandwich made with peanut butter! The sensation is simply unexplainable. You just have to try it yourself.

Serving Size: Makes 1 serving.

List of Ingredients:

- 3 tablespoons peanut butter
- 1 teaspoon maple syrup
- Cinnamon
- 2 slices of bread
- 1 banana
- 1 green apple

MMMMMMMMMMMMMMMMMMMMMMMMMMMMMMMMM

Instructions:

1. 2 slices of bread

2. 1 banana

3. 1 green apple

4. 3 tablespoons peanut butter

5. 1 teaspoon maple syrup cinnamon

6. Toast the bread and thinly slice the fruits (sprinkle fruit with lemon juice if you want to prepare it for the next day, so it won't get brown).

7. Rub the peanut butter on both bread slices, layer fruits, pour with maple syrup and then sprinkle with the cinnamon.

(49) Red Leaf Lettuce Sandwich

Red Leaf Lettuce naturally is a calorie free food. Blending it with kalamata olives makes it a super food. Ensure the measurements are adhered to strictly to get the best from this.

Serving Size: Makes 2 serving.

List of Ingredients:

- 2 tablespoons your favorite Pesto
- 4 (¼ " thick) slices of Sourdough Bread
- ½ cup minced Kalamata Olives
- 4 Tomato slices
- Red Leaf Lettuce

MMMMMMMMMMMMMMMMMMMMMMMMMMMMMMMMMM

Instructions:

1. Toast the bread spreading a tablespoon of pesto on one slice and spread half of the minced olives on the other side.

2. Put the tomatoes on top of the olives and add lettuce with the red onion on it; Layer all of them together with your pesto slice.

(50) Nutty Chickpea Salad Sandwich

The taste of the flaked chickpeas is extremely incredible. It has the aroma and texture reminds of a tuna salad sandwich. You should get your teeth in this.

Serving Size: Makes 6 serving.

List of Ingredients:

- 2 stalks of celery; washed and finely chopped
- ½ cup of chopped blanched almonds or walnuts
- 1 tablespoon of dijon mustard
- ½ cup of mayonnaise without eggs or low-fat mayonnaise
- 2-15 ounce cans of chickpeas which have been rinsed and drained
- 1 finely chopped red pepper
- 2 peeled and grated carrots
- 2 tablespoons of fresh chopped herbs
- Salt & pepper

MMMMMMMMMMMMMMMMMMMMMMMMMMMMMMMMMM

Instructions:

1. Put the drained chickpeas in a food processor and pulse them for 6 times. Prevent turning the chickpeas into a paste or a purée so as to have them flake a bit.

2. Mix the mayonnaise with the dijon mustard, pepper and salt. Put the grated carrots, almonds, chickpeas or walnuts, chopped celery and pepper into it. Drizzle the fresh chopped herb in it and mix well.

3. Put the spread on any whole grain bread and add some thin diced radishes.

About the Author

A native of Indianapolis, Indiana, Valeria Ray found her passion for cooking while she was studying English Literature at Oakland City University. She decided to try a cooking course with her friends and the experience changed her forever. She enrolled at the Art Institute of Indiana which offered extensive courses in the culinary Arts. Once Ray dipped her toe in the cooking world, she never looked back.

When Valeria graduated, she worked in French restaurants in the Indianapolis area until she became the head chef at one of the 5-star establishments in the area. Valeria's attention to taste and visual detail caught the eye of a local business person who expressed an interest in publishing her recipes. Valeria began her secondary career authoring cookbooks and e-books which she tackled with as much talent and gusto as her first career. Her passion for food leaps off the page of her books which have colourful anecdotes and stunning pictures of dishes she has prepared herself.

Valeria Ray lives in Indianapolis with her husband of 15 years, Tom, her daughter, Isobel and their loveable Golden Retriever, Goldy. Valeria enjoys cooking special dishes in her large, comfortable kitchen where the family gets involved in preparing meals. This successful, dynamic chef is an inspiration to culinary students and novice cooks everywhere.

••••••••• ● ● ● ● ● ● •••••

Author's Afterthoughts

Thank you for Purchasing my book and taking the time to read it from front to back. I am always grateful when a reader chooses my work and I hope you enjoyed it!

With the vast selection available online, I am touched that you chose to be purchasing my work and take valuable time out of your life to read it. My hope is that you feel you made the right decision.

I very much would like to know what you thought of the book. Please take the time to write an honest and informative review on Amazon.com. Your experience and opinions will be of great benefit to me and those readers looking to make an informed choice.

With much thanks,

Valeria Ray

Printed in Great Britain
by Amazon